Designed to Be You Series

GOD IS ALWAYS WITH YOU
AN ADVENTURE!

BY BETO PEÑA
ILLUSTRATIONS BY NEVA HARRISON

GOD IS ALWAYS WITH YOU
AN ADVENTURE!

Story copyright © 2017 by Beto Peña
Illustrations copyright © 2017 by Neva Harrison
Layout: Ryan Richey
All rights reserved. Published by Beto Peña
ISBN-13: 978-0-9909980-3-7   ISBN-10: 0-9909980-3-7

For All of God's Children.

*Thank you to my princess, Gina, and to all of you who offered invaluable input.

Scripture quotations marked (ERV) are taken from the Holy Bible: Easy-to-Read VersionTM (ERVTM) © 1987, 2004 by Bible League International and used by permission.

Scripture quotations marked (GNT) are from the Good News Translation in Today's English Version- Second Edition Copyright © 1992 by American Bible Society. Used by Permission.

Scripture quotations marked (GW) are taken from GOD'S WORD®, © 1995 God's Word to the Nations. Used by permission of Baker Publishing Group.

Scripture quotations marked (ICB) are taken from the The Holy Bible, International Children's Bible® Copyright© 1986, 1988, 1999, 2015 by Tommy Nelson™, a division of Thomas Nelson. Used by permission.

Scripture quotations marked (NIV) are taken from the Holy Bible, New International Version®, NIV® Copyright © 1973, 1978, 1984, 2011 by Biblica, Inc.® Used by permission. All rights reserved worldwide.

Scripture quotations marked (NIRV) are taken from the Holy Bible, NEW INTERNATIONAL READER'S VERSION®. Copyright © 1996, 1998 Biblica. All rights reserved throughout the world. Used by permission of Biblica.

Scriptures quotations marked (NCV) taken from the New Century Version®. Copyright © 2005 by Thomas Nelson. Used by permission. All rights reserved.

Scripture quotations marked (NLT) are taken from the Holy Bible, New Living Translation, copyright ©1996, 2004, 2007, 2013, 2015 by Tyndale House Foundation. Used by permission of Tyndale House Publishers, Inc., Carol Stream, Illinois 60188. All rights reserved.

No part of this publication may be reproduced, stored in a retrieval system, or transmitted in any form or by any means, electronic, mechanical, photocopying, recording, or otherwise, without written permission of the author. For information regarding permission, please email BetoPena@yahoo.com

An UNEXPECTED journey!

God has taken the book, God's Plan Just for You!, in the Designed to Be You Series, to Europe, Africa, South America, and Asia, so far! My vision for that first book was simply a Christmas gift for my son, yet it has been translated into various languages and is just the beginning for this series (Lord willing). Whether young or old, my prayer is that you catch the vision of what it means to have a personal relationship with God, through His Son, Jesus, and His wonderful journey as you enjoy Him enjoying you! Happy reading!

DESIGNED TO BE YOU SERIES TITLES & THEMES!

A Place in God's Family for You!

God's Protection All Around You!

The Mightiness of God!

Names of God Just for You!

When Hurt Happens!

What is Your Giant?

As your Heavenly Father, He's always with you!

He knows what you're thinking, and all you will say.

You know everything I do; from far away You understand all my thoughts. Even before I speak, You already know what I will say.   Psalm 139:2 & 4 (GNT)

He's there when you're sitting, and when you go play.

YES, GOD KNOWS ALL ABOUT YOU, JUST BECAUSE HE CARES.

Lord, You have examined me, and You know me.
Psalm 139:1 (ICB)

So let's go on an ADVENTURE and see that it's true,

The Bible will show us, God's ALWAYS with you!

Wherever you are,

He's ALREADY there.

Your Spirit is everywhere I go. I cannot escape from Your presence. Psalm 139:7 (ERV)

PRETEND YOU COULD SOAR LIKE A BIRD SO HIGH,

If I go up to the heavens, You are there.
Psalm 139:8a (NIRV)

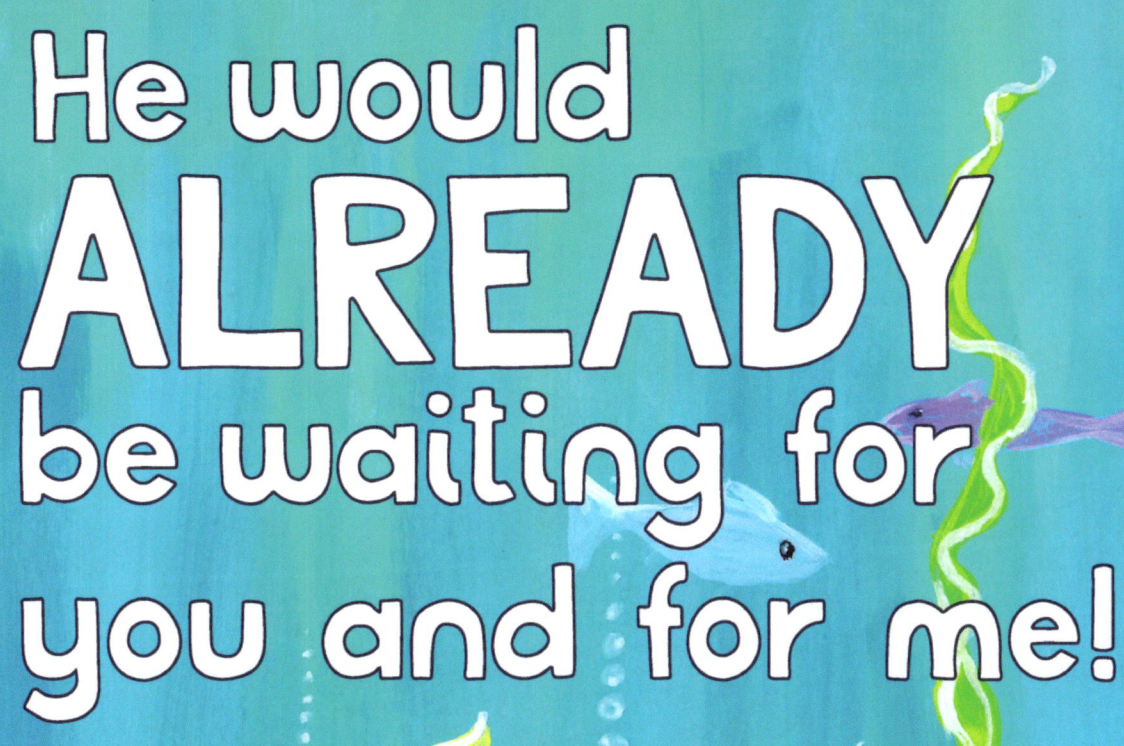

He would ALREADY be waiting for you and for me!

If I lie down in the deepest parts of the earth, You are also there.
Psalm 139:8b (NIRV)

Or say you could ride on the RAYS of the sun,

He would be there too! Wouldn't that be FUN?!

If I rise on the wings of the dawn... even there
Your hand will guide me...
Psalms 139:9-10 (NIV)

He sees in the DARK as though it were LIGHT,

...even in darkness I cannot hide from You.
To You the night shines as bright as day.
Darkness & light are the same to You.
Psalm 139:12 (NLT)

because nothing is hidden from his eyesight.

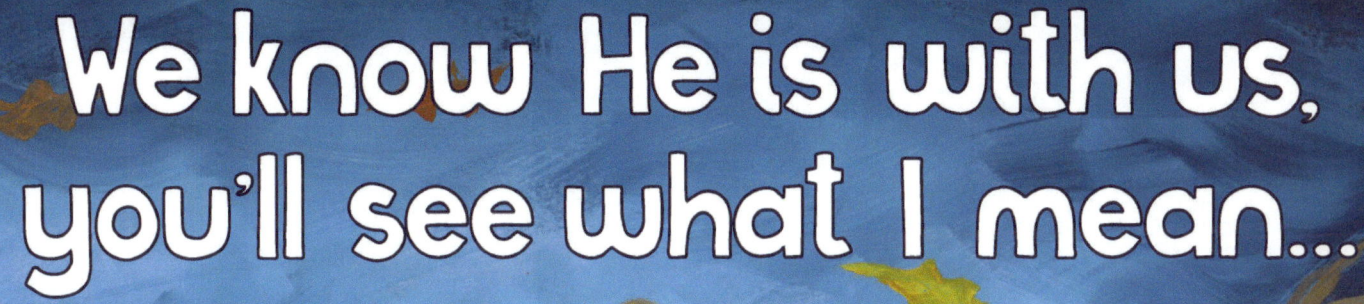

...Through everything God made, they can clearly see
His invisible qualities—
His eternal power and divine nature.
Romans 1:20 (NLT)

Who made the earth,

the stars, and the sea?

We see all His work, it's clear as can be!

God created the heavens and stretched them out;
He fashioned the earth and all that lives there;
He gave life and breath to all its people.

Isaiah 42:5 (GNT)

And before YOU were born,

HE made every part,

and even when you're HAPPY, He wants You to know...

Don't worry, because I am with you. Don't be afraid, because I am your God. I will make you strong and will help you. Isaiah 41:10 (ICB)

on the path I'll lead you,

all along the way.

Why does He promise to stay by our side?

I will instruct you and teach you in the way you should go;
I will counsel you with my loving eye on you.
Psalm 32:8 (NIV)

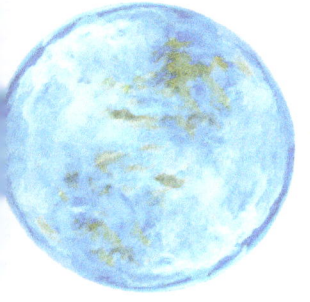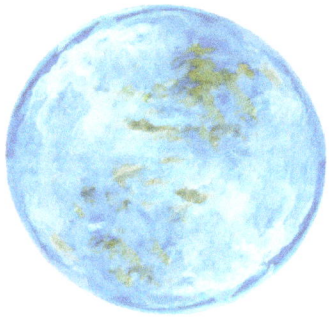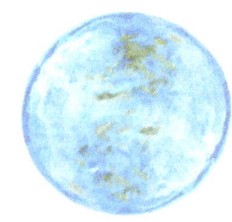

GOD IS ALWAYS WITH YOU: AN ADVENTURE!
Creators

Beto has been involved in ministry since 2001, serving most of those years as a children's pastor, and has a knack for relating to kids on their level. Having a Master's Degree in Counseling, his passion lies in helping others discover who they are in Christ, what their God-given purpose is, and how to live out that purpose daily. Beto currently lives in Boerne, Texas with his wife and son.

Born in California in 1948, Neva discovered her passion for art at the age of 5. Travels through the Western states and a sense of wonder drove her to develop her self-taught, God-given gift with excitement and adventure. Though having done commission work for 40 years, she leans more towards creating from her imagination and plans on painting and enjoying life with all it's beauty until the end.